## This Planner Belongs To:

Name: _____

Phone: _____

Address: _____

Email: _____

## Emergency contact:

Name: _____

Phone: _____

Address: _____

Email: _____

Copyright ©2018
Ritchie Media
Peterborough, ON, Canada

# 2018

## January
| M | T | W | T | F | S | S |
|---|---|---|---|---|---|---|
| 1 | 2 | 3 | 4 | 5 | 6 | 7 |
| 8 | 9 | 10 | 11 | 12 | 13 | 14 |
| 15 | 16 | 17 | 18 | 19 | 20 | 21 |
| 22 | 23 | 24 | 25 | 26 | 27 | 28 |
| 29 | 30 | 31 | | | | |

## February
| M | T | W | T | F | S | S |
|---|---|---|---|---|---|---|
| | | | 1 | 2 | 3 | 4 |
| 5 | 6 | 7 | 8 | 9 | 10 | 11 |
| 12 | 13 | 14 | 15 | 16 | 17 | 18 |
| 19 | 20 | 21 | 22 | 23 | 24 | 25 |
| 26 | 27 | 28 | | | | |

## March
| M | T | W | T | F | S | S |
|---|---|---|---|---|---|---|
| | | | 1 | 2 | 3 | 4 |
| 5 | 6 | 7 | 8 | 9 | 10 | 11 |
| 12 | 13 | 14 | 15 | 16 | 17 | 18 |
| 19 | 20 | 21 | 22 | 23 | 24 | 25 |
| 26 | 27 | 28 | 29 | 30 | 31 | |

## April
| M | T | W | T | F | S | S |
|---|---|---|---|---|---|---|
| | | | | | | 1 |
| 2 | 3 | 4 | 5 | 6 | 7 | 8 |
| 9 | 10 | 11 | 12 | 13 | 14 | 15 |
| 16 | 17 | 18 | 19 | 20 | 21 | 22 |
| 23 | 24 | 25 | 26 | 27 | 28 | 29 |
| 30 | | | | | | |

## May
| M | T | W | T | F | S | S |
|---|---|---|---|---|---|---|
| | 1 | 2 | 3 | 4 | 5 | 6 |
| 7 | 8 | 9 | 10 | 11 | 12 | 13 |
| 14 | 15 | 16 | 17 | 18 | 19 | 20 |
| 21 | 22 | 23 | 24 | 25 | 26 | 27 |
| 28 | 29 | 30 | 31 | | | |

## June
| M | T | W | T | F | S | S |
|---|---|---|---|---|---|---|
| | | | | 1 | 2 | 3 |
| 4 | 5 | 6 | 7 | 8 | 9 | 10 |
| 11 | 12 | 13 | 14 | 15 | 16 | 17 |
| 18 | 19 | 20 | 21 | 22 | 23 | 24 |
| 25 | 26 | 27 | 28 | 29 | 30 | |

## July
| M | T | W | T | F | S | S |
|---|---|---|---|---|---|---|
| | | | | | | 1 |
| 2 | 3 | 4 | 5 | 6 | 7 | 8 |
| 9 | 10 | 11 | 12 | 13 | 14 | 15 |
| 16 | 17 | 18 | 19 | 20 | 21 | 22 |
| 23 | 24 | 25 | 26 | 27 | 28 | 29 |
| 30 | 31 | | | | | |

## August
| M | T | W | T | F | S | S |
|---|---|---|---|---|---|---|
| | | 1 | 2 | 3 | 4 | 5 |
| 6 | 7 | 8 | 9 | 10 | 11 | 12 |
| 13 | 14 | 15 | 16 | 17 | 18 | 19 |
| 20 | 21 | 22 | 23 | 24 | 25 | 26 |
| 27 | 28 | 29 | 30 | 31 | | |

## September
| M | T | W | T | F | S | S |
|---|---|---|---|---|---|---|
| | | | | | 1 | 2 |
| 3 | 4 | 5 | 6 | 7 | 8 | 9 |
| 10 | 11 | 12 | 13 | 14 | 15 | 16 |
| 17 | 18 | 19 | 20 | 21 | 22 | 23 |
| 24 | 25 | 26 | 27 | 28 | 29 | 30 |

## October
| M | T | W | T | F | S | S |
|---|---|---|---|---|---|---|
| 1 | 2 | 3 | 4 | 5 | 6 | 7 |
| 8 | 9 | 10 | 11 | 12 | 13 | 14 |
| 15 | 16 | 17 | 18 | 19 | 20 | 21 |
| 22 | 23 | 24 | 25 | 26 | 27 | 28 |
| 29 | 30 | 31 | | | | |

## November
| M | T | W | T | F | S | S |
|---|---|---|---|---|---|---|
| | | | 1 | 2 | 3 | 4 |
| 5 | 6 | 7 | 8 | 9 | 10 | 11 |
| 12 | 13 | 14 | 15 | 16 | 17 | 18 |
| 19 | 20 | 21 | 22 | 23 | 24 | 25 |
| 26 | 27 | 28 | 29 | 30 | | |

## December
| M | T | W | T | F | S | S |
|---|---|---|---|---|---|---|
| | | | | | 1 | 2 |
| 3 | 4 | 5 | 6 | 7 | 8 | 9 |
| 10 | 11 | 12 | 13 | 14 | 15 | 16 |
| 17 | 18 | 19 | 20 | 21 | 22 | 23 |
| 24 | 25 | 26 | 27 | 28 | 29 | 30 |
| 31 | | | | | | |

# 2019

## January
| M | T | W | T | F | S | S |
|---|---|---|---|---|---|---|
| 31 | 1 | 2 | 3 | 4 | 5 | 6 |
| 7 | 8 | 9 | 10 | 11 | 12 | 13 |
| 14 | 15 | 16 | 17 | 18 | 19 | 20 |
| 21 | 22 | 23 | 24 | 25 | 26 | 27 |
| 28 | 29 | 30 | 31 | 1 | 2 | 3 |
| 4 | 5 | 6 | 7 | 8 | 9 | 10 |

## February
| M | T | W | T | F | S | S |
|---|---|---|---|---|---|---|
| 28 | 29 | 30 | 31 | 1 | 2 | 3 |
| 4 | 5 | 6 | 7 | 8 | 9 | 10 |
| 11 | 12 | 13 | 14 | 15 | 16 | 17 |
| 18 | 19 | 20 | 21 | 22 | 23 | 24 |
| 25 | 26 | 27 | 28 | 1 | 2 | 3 |
| 4 | 5 | 6 | 7 | 8 | 9 | 10 |

## March
| M | T | W | T | F | S | S |
|---|---|---|---|---|---|---|
| 25 | 26 | 27 | 28 | 1 | 2 | 3 |
| 4 | 5 | 6 | 7 | 8 | 9 | 10 |
| 11 | 12 | 13 | 14 | 15 | 16 | 17 |
| 18 | 19 | 20 | 21 | 22 | 23 | 24 |
| 25 | 26 | 27 | 28 | 29 | 30 | 31 |
| 1 | 2 | 3 | 4 | 5 | 6 | 7 |

## April
| M | T | W | T | F | S | S |
|---|---|---|---|---|---|---|
| 1 | 2 | 3 | 4 | 5 | 6 | 7 |
| 8 | 9 | 10 | 11 | 12 | 13 | 14 |
| 15 | 16 | 17 | 18 | 19 | 20 | 21 |
| 22 | 23 | 24 | 25 | 26 | 27 | 28 |
| 29 | 30 | 1 | 2 | 3 | 4 | 5 |
| 6 | 7 | 8 | 9 | 10 | 11 | 12 |

## May
| M | T | W | T | F | S | S |
|---|---|---|---|---|---|---|
| 29 | 30 | 1 | 2 | 3 | 4 | 5 |
| 6 | 7 | 8 | 9 | 10 | 11 | 12 |
| 13 | 14 | 15 | 16 | 17 | 18 | 19 |
| 20 | 21 | 22 | 23 | 24 | 25 | 26 |
| 27 | 28 | 29 | 30 | 31 | 1 | 2 |
| 3 | 4 | 5 | 6 | 7 | 8 | 9 |

## June
| M | T | W | T | F | S | S |
|---|---|---|---|---|---|---|
| 27 | 28 | 29 | 30 | 31 | 1 | 2 |
| 3 | 4 | 5 | 6 | 7 | 8 | 9 |
| 10 | 11 | 12 | 13 | 14 | 15 | 16 |
| 17 | 18 | 19 | 20 | 21 | 22 | 23 |
| 24 | 25 | 26 | 27 | 28 | 29 | 30 |
| 1 | 2 | 3 | 4 | 5 | 6 | 7 |

## July
| M | T | W | T | F | S | S |
|---|---|---|---|---|---|---|
| 1 | 2 | 3 | 4 | 5 | 6 | 7 |
| 8 | 9 | 10 | 11 | 12 | 13 | 14 |
| 15 | 16 | 17 | 18 | 19 | 20 | 21 |
| 22 | 23 | 24 | 25 | 26 | 27 | 28 |
| 29 | 30 | 31 | 1 | 2 | 3 | 4 |
| 5 | 6 | 7 | 8 | 9 | 10 | 11 |

## August
| M | T | W | T | F | S | S |
|---|---|---|---|---|---|---|
| 29 | 30 | 31 | 1 | 2 | 3 | 4 |
| 5 | 6 | 7 | 8 | 9 | 10 | 11 |
| 12 | 13 | 14 | 15 | 16 | 17 | 18 |
| 19 | 20 | 21 | 22 | 23 | 24 | 25 |
| 26 | 27 | 28 | 29 | 30 | 31 | 1 |
| 2 | 3 | 4 | 5 | 6 | 7 | 8 |

## September
| M | T | W | T | F | S | S |
|---|---|---|---|---|---|---|
| 26 | 27 | 28 | 29 | 30 | 31 | 1 |
| 2 | 3 | 4 | 5 | 6 | 7 | 8 |
| 9 | 10 | 11 | 12 | 13 | 14 | 15 |
| 16 | 17 | 18 | 19 | 20 | 21 | 22 |
| 23 | 24 | 25 | 26 | 27 | 28 | 29 |
| 30 | 1 | 2 | 3 | 4 | 5 | 6 |

## October
| M | T | W | T | F | S | S |
|---|---|---|---|---|---|---|
| 30 | 1 | 2 | 3 | 4 | 5 | 6 |
| 7 | 8 | 9 | 10 | 11 | 12 | 13 |
| 14 | 15 | 16 | 17 | 18 | 19 | 20 |
| 21 | 22 | 23 | 24 | 25 | 26 | 27 |
| 28 | 29 | 30 | 31 | 1 | 2 | 3 |
| 4 | 5 | 6 | 7 | 8 | 9 | 10 |

## November
| M | T | W | T | F | S | S |
|---|---|---|---|---|---|---|
| 28 | 29 | 30 | 31 | 1 | 2 | 3 |
| 4 | 5 | 6 | 7 | 8 | 9 | 10 |
| 11 | 12 | 13 | 14 | 15 | 16 | 17 |
| 18 | 19 | 20 | 21 | 22 | 23 | 24 |
| 25 | 26 | 27 | 28 | 29 | 30 | 1 |
| 2 | 3 | 4 | 5 | 6 | 7 | 8 |

## December
| M | T | W | T | F | S | S |
|---|---|---|---|---|---|---|
| 25 | 26 | 27 | 28 | 29 | 30 | 1 |
| 2 | 3 | 4 | 5 | 6 | 7 | 8 |
| 9 | 10 | 11 | 12 | 13 | 14 | 15 |
| 16 | 17 | 18 | 19 | 20 | 21 | 22 |
| 23 | 24 | 25 | 26 | 27 | 28 | 29 |
| 30 | 31 | 1 | 2 | 3 | 4 | 5 |

# Important Contacts

Name:

Phone:

Address:

Email:

Name:

Phone:

Address:

Email:

Name:

Phone:

Address:

Email:

Name:

Phone:

Address:

Email:

Name:

Phone:

Address:

Email:

# Notes

# Week of: _____

| Monday | | Morning | | Afternoon | | Evening |
|---|---|---|---|---|---|---|
| | 8:00 | | 1:00 | | 6:00 | |
| | 9:00 | | 2:00 | | 7:00 | |
| | 10:00 | | 3:00 | | 8:00 | |
| | 11:00 | | 4:00 | | 9:00 | |
| | 12:00 | | 5:00 | | 10:00 | |

Notes:

Priorities:

| Tuesday | | Morning | | Afternoon | | Evening |
|---|---|---|---|---|---|---|
| | 8:00 | | 1:00 | | 6:00 | |
| | 9:00 | | 2:00 | | 7:00 | |
| | 10:00 | | 3:00 | | 8:00 | |
| | 11:00 | | 4:00 | | 9:00 | |
| | 12:00 | | 5:00 | | 10:00 | |

Notes:

Priorities:

| Wednesday | | Morning | | Afternoon | | Evening |
|---|---|---|---|---|---|---|
| | 8:00 | | 1:00 | | 6:00 | |
| | 9:00 | | 2:00 | | 7:00 | |
| | 10:00 | | 3:00 | | 8:00 | |
| | 11:00 | | 4:00 | | 9:00 | |
| | 12:00 | | 5:00 | | 10:00 | |

Notes:

Priorities:

| Thursday | | Morning | | Afternoon | | Evening |
|---|---|---|---|---|---|---|
| | 8:00 | | 1:00 | | 6:00 | |
| | 9:00 | | 2:00 | | 7:00 | |
| | 10:00 | | 3:00 | | 8:00 | |
| | 11:00 | | 4:00 | | 9:00 | |
| | 12:00 | | 5:00 | | 10:00 | |

Notes:

Priorities:

| Friday | | Morning | | Afternoon | | Evening |
|---|---|---|---|---|---|---|
| | 8:00 | | 1:00 | | 6:00 | |
| | 9:00 | | 2:00 | | 7:00 | |
| | 10:00 | | 3:00 | | 8:00 | |
| | 11:00 | | 4:00 | | 9:00 | |
| | 12:00 | | 5:00 | | 10:00 | |

Notes:

Priorities:

| Weekend | | Morning | | Afternoon | | Evening |
|---|---|---|---|---|---|---|
| | 8:00 | | 1:00 | | 6:00 | |
| | 9:00 | | 2:00 | | 7:00 | |
| | 10:00 | | 3:00 | | 8:00 | |
| | 11:00 | | 4:00 | | 9:00 | |
| | 12:00 | | 5:00 | | 10:00 | |

Notes:

Priorities:

# Notes

Week of: _____

| Monday | | Morning | | Afternoon | | Evening | |
|---|---|---|---|---|---|---|---|
| | 8:00 | | 1:00 | | 6:00 | | |
| | 9:00 | | 2:00 | | 7:00 | | |
| | 10:00 | | 3:00 | | 8:00 | | |
| | 11:00 | | 4:00 | | 9:00 | | |
| | 12:00 | | 5:00 | | 10:00 | | |

Notes:

Priorities:

| Tuesday | | Morning | | Afternoon | | Evening | |
|---|---|---|---|---|---|---|---|
| | 8:00 | | 1:00 | | 6:00 | | |
| | 9:00 | | 2:00 | | 7:00 | | |
| | 10:00 | | 3:00 | | 8:00 | | |
| | 11:00 | | 4:00 | | 9:00 | | |
| | 12:00 | | 5:00 | | 10:00 | | |

Notes:

Priorities:

| Wednesday | | Morning | | Afternoon | | Evening | |
|---|---|---|---|---|---|---|---|
| | 8:00 | | 1:00 | | 6:00 | | |
| | 9:00 | | 2:00 | | 7:00 | | |
| | 10:00 | | 3:00 | | 8:00 | | |
| | 11:00 | | 4:00 | | 9:00 | | |
| | 12:00 | | 5:00 | | 10:00 | | |

Notes:

Priorities:

| Thursday | | Morning | | Afternoon | | Evening | |
|---|---|---|---|---|---|---|---|
| | 8:00 | | 1:00 | | 6:00 | | |
| | 9:00 | | 2:00 | | 7:00 | | |
| | 10:00 | | 3:00 | | 8:00 | | |
| | 11:00 | | 4:00 | | 9:00 | | |
| | 12:00 | | 5:00 | | 10:00 | | |

Notes:

Priorities:

| Friday | | Morning | | Afternoon | | Evening |
|---|---|---|---|---|---|---|
| | 8:00 | | 1:00 | | 6:00 | |
| | 9:00 | | 2:00 | | 7:00 | |
| | 10:00 | | 3:00 | | 8:00 | |
| | 11:00 | | 4:00 | | 9:00 | |
| | 12:00 | | 5:00 | | 10:00 | |

Notes:

Priorities:

| Weekend | | Morning | | Afternoon | | Evening |
|---|---|---|---|---|---|---|
| | 8:00 | | 1:00 | | 6:00 | |
| | 9:00 | | 2:00 | | 7:00 | |
| | 10:00 | | 3:00 | | 8:00 | |
| | 11:00 | | 4:00 | | 9:00 | |
| | 12:00 | | 5:00 | | 10:00 | |

Notes:

Priorities:

# Notes

# Week of: _____

| Monday | | Morning | | Afternoon | | Evening |
|---|---|---|---|---|---|---|
| | 8:00 | | 1:00 | | 6:00 | |
| | 9:00 | | 2:00 | | 7:00 | |
| | 10:00 | | 3:00 | | 8:00 | |
| | 11:00 | | 4:00 | | 9:00 | |
| | 12:00 | | 5:00 | | 10:00 | |

Notes:

Priorities:

| Tuesday | | Morning | | Afternoon | | Evening |
|---|---|---|---|---|---|---|
| | 8:00 | | 1:00 | | 6:00 | |
| | 9:00 | | 2:00 | | 7:00 | |
| | 10:00 | | 3:00 | | 8:00 | |
| | 11:00 | | 4:00 | | 9:00 | |
| | 12:00 | | 5:00 | | 10:00 | |

Notes:

Priorities:

| Wednesday | | Morning | | Afternoon | | Evening |
|---|---|---|---|---|---|---|
| | 8:00 | | 1:00 | | 6:00 | |
| | 9:00 | | 2:00 | | 7:00 | |
| | 10:00 | | 3:00 | | 8:00 | |
| | 11:00 | | 4:00 | | 9:00 | |
| | 12:00 | | 5:00 | | 10:00 | |

**Notes:**

**Priorities:**

| Thursday | | Morning | | Afternoon | | Evening |
|---|---|---|---|---|---|---|
| | 8:00 | | 1:00 | | 6:00 | |
| | 9:00 | | 2:00 | | 7:00 | |
| | 10:00 | | 3:00 | | 8:00 | |
| | 11:00 | | 4:00 | | 9:00 | |
| | 12:00 | | 5:00 | | 10:00 | |

**Notes:**

**Priorities:**

| Friday | | Morning | | Afternoon | | Evening |
|---|---|---|---|---|---|---|
| | 8:00 | | 1:00 | | 6:00 | |
| | 9:00 | | 2:00 | | 7:00 | |
| | 10:00 | | 3:00 | | 8:00 | |
| | 11:00 | | 4:00 | | 9:00 | |
| | 12:00 | | 5:00 | | 10:00 | |

Notes:

Priorities:

| Weekend | | Morning | | Afternoon | | Evening |
|---|---|---|---|---|---|---|
| | 8:00 | | 1:00 | | 6:00 | |
| | 9:00 | | 2:00 | | 7:00 | |
| | 10:00 | | 3:00 | | 8:00 | |
| | 11:00 | | 4:00 | | 9:00 | |
| | 12:00 | | 5:00 | | 10:00 | |

Notes:

Priorities:

# Notes

# Week of: _____

| Monday | | Morning | | Afternoon | | Evening | |
|---|---|---|---|---|---|---|---|
| | 8:00 | | 1:00 | | 6:00 | | |
| | 9:00 | | 2:00 | | 7:00 | | |
| | 10:00 | | 3:00 | | 8:00 | | |
| | 11:00 | | 4:00 | | 9:00 | | |
| | 12:00 | | 5:00 | | 10:00 | | |

**Notes:**

**Priorities:**

| Tuesday | | Morning | | Afternoon | | Evening | |
|---|---|---|---|---|---|---|---|
| | 8:00 | | 1:00 | | 6:00 | | |
| | 9:00 | | 2:00 | | 7:00 | | |
| | 10:00 | | 3:00 | | 8:00 | | |
| | 11:00 | | 4:00 | | 9:00 | | |
| | 12:00 | | 5:00 | | 10:00 | | |

**Notes:**

**Priorities:**

| Wednesday | | Morning | | Afternoon | | Evening |
|---|---|---|---|---|---|---|
| | 8:00 | | 1:00 | | 6:00 | |
| | 9:00 | | 2:00 | | 7:00 | |
| | 10:00 | | 3:00 | | 8:00 | |
| | 11:00 | | 4:00 | | 9:00 | |
| | 12:00 | | 5:00 | | 10:00 | |

Notes:

Priorities:

| Thursday | | Morning | | Afternoon | | Evening |
|---|---|---|---|---|---|---|
| | 8:00 | | 1:00 | | 6:00 | |
| | 9:00 | | 2:00 | | 7:00 | |
| | 10:00 | | 3:00 | | 8:00 | |
| | 11:00 | | 4:00 | | 9:00 | |
| | 12:00 | | 5:00 | | 10:00 | |

Notes:

Priorities:

| Friday | | Morning | | Afternoon | | Evening |
|---|---|---|---|---|---|---|
| | 8:00 | | 1:00 | | 6:00 | |
| | 9:00 | | 2:00 | | 7:00 | |
| | 10:00 | | 3:00 | | 8:00 | |
| | 11:00 | | 4:00 | | 9:00 | |
| | 12:00 | | 5:00 | | 10:00 | |

Notes:

Priorities:

| Weekend | | Morning | | Afternoon | | Evening |
|---|---|---|---|---|---|---|
| | 8:00 | | 1:00 | | 6:00 | |
| | 9:00 | | 2:00 | | 7:00 | |
| | 10:00 | | 3:00 | | 8:00 | |
| | 11:00 | | 4:00 | | 9:00 | |
| | 12:00 | | 5:00 | | 10:00 | |

Notes:

Priorities:

# Notes

# Week of: _____

| Monday | | Morning | | Afternoon | | Evening | |
|---|---|---|---|---|---|---|---|
| | 8:00 | | 1:00 | | 6:00 | | |
| | 9:00 | | 2:00 | | 7:00 | | |
| | 10:00 | | 3:00 | | 8:00 | | |
| | 11:00 | | 4:00 | | 9:00 | | |
| | 12:00 | | 5:00 | | 10:00 | | |

**Notes:**

**Priorities:**

| Tuesday | | Morning | | Afternoon | | Evening | |
|---|---|---|---|---|---|---|---|
| | 8:00 | | 1:00 | | 6:00 | | |
| | 9:00 | | 2:00 | | 7:00 | | |
| | 10:00 | | 3:00 | | 8:00 | | |
| | 11:00 | | 4:00 | | 9:00 | | |
| | 12:00 | | 5:00 | | 10:00 | | |

**Notes:**

**Priorities:**

| Wednesday | | Morning | | Afternoon | | Evening |
|---|---|---|---|---|---|---|
| | 8:00 | | 1:00 | | 6:00 | |
| | 9:00 | | 2:00 | | 7:00 | |
| | 10:00 | | 3:00 | | 8:00 | |
| | 11:00 | | 4:00 | | 9:00 | |
| | 12:00 | | 5:00 | | 10:00 | |

Notes:

Priorities:

| Thursday | | Morning | | Afternoon | | Evening |
|---|---|---|---|---|---|---|
| | 8:00 | | 1:00 | | 6:00 | |
| | 9:00 | | 2:00 | | 7:00 | |
| | 10:00 | | 3:00 | | 8:00 | |
| | 11:00 | | 4:00 | | 9:00 | |
| | 12:00 | | 5:00 | | 10:00 | |

Notes:

Priorities:

| Friday | | Morning | | Afternoon | | Evening |
|---|---|---|---|---|---|---|
| | 8:00 | | 1:00 | | 6:00 | |
| | 9:00 | | 2:00 | | 7:00 | |
| | 10:00 | | 3:00 | | 8:00 | |
| | 11:00 | | 4:00 | | 9:00 | |
| | 12:00 | | 5:00 | | 10:00 | |

Notes:

Priorities:

| Weekend | | Morning | | Afternoon | | Evening |
|---|---|---|---|---|---|---|
| | 8:00 | | 1:00 | | 6:00 | |
| | 9:00 | | 2:00 | | 7:00 | |
| | 10:00 | | 3:00 | | 8:00 | |
| | 11:00 | | 4:00 | | 9:00 | |
| | 12:00 | | 5:00 | | 10:00 | |

Notes:

Priorities:

# Notes

# Week of: _____

| Monday | | Morning | | Afternoon | | Evening |
|---|---|---|---|---|---|---|
| | 8:00 | | 1:00 | | 6:00 | |
| | 9:00 | | 2:00 | | 7:00 | |
| | 10:00 | | 3:00 | | 8:00 | |
| | 11:00 | | 4:00 | | 9:00 | |
| | 12:00 | | 5:00 | | 10:00 | |

**Notes:**

**Priorities:**

| Tuesday | | Morning | | Afternoon | | Evening |
|---|---|---|---|---|---|---|
| | 8:00 | | 1:00 | | 6:00 | |
| | 9:00 | | 2:00 | | 7:00 | |
| | 10:00 | | 3:00 | | 8:00 | |
| | 11:00 | | 4:00 | | 9:00 | |
| | 12:00 | | 5:00 | | 10:00 | |

**Notes:**

**Priorities:**

| Wednesday | | Morning | | Afternoon | | Evening |
|---|---|---|---|---|---|---|
| | 8:00 | | 1:00 | | 6:00 | |
| | 9:00 | | 2:00 | | 7:00 | |
| | 10:00 | | 3:00 | | 8:00 | |
| | 11:00 | | 4:00 | | 9:00 | |
| | 12:00 | | 5:00 | | 10:00 | |

Notes:

Priorities:

| Thursday | | Morning | | Afternoon | | Evening |
|---|---|---|---|---|---|---|
| | 8:00 | | 1:00 | | 6:00 | |
| | 9:00 | | 2:00 | | 7:00 | |
| | 10:00 | | 3:00 | | 8:00 | |
| | 11:00 | | 4:00 | | 9:00 | |
| | 12:00 | | 5:00 | | 10:00 | |

Notes:

Priorities:

| Friday | | Morning | | Afternoon | | Evening |
|---|---|---|---|---|---|---|
| | 8:00 | | 1:00 | | 6:00 | |
| | 9:00 | | 2:00 | | 7:00 | |
| | 10:00 | | 3:00 | | 8:00 | |
| | 11:00 | | 4:00 | | 9:00 | |
| | 12:00 | | 5:00 | | 10:00 | |

Notes:

Priorities:

| Weekend | | Morning | | Afternoon | | Evening |
|---|---|---|---|---|---|---|
| | 8:00 | | 1:00 | | 6:00 | |
| | 9:00 | | 2:00 | | 7:00 | |
| | 10:00 | | 3:00 | | 8:00 | |
| | 11:00 | | 4:00 | | 9:00 | |
| | 12:00 | | 5:00 | | 10:00 | |

Notes:

Priorities:

# Notes

# Week of: _____

| Monday | | Morning | | Afternoon | | Evening |
|---|---|---|---|---|---|---|
| | 8:00 | | 1:00 | | 6:00 | |
| | 9:00 | | 2:00 | | 7:00 | |
| | 10:00 | | 3:00 | | 8:00 | |
| | 11:00 | | 4:00 | | 9:00 | |
| | 12:00 | | 5:00 | | 10:00 | |

Notes:

Priorities:

| Tuesday | | Morning | | Afternoon | | Evening |
|---|---|---|---|---|---|---|
| | 8:00 | | 1:00 | | 6:00 | |
| | 9:00 | | 2:00 | | 7:00 | |
| | 10:00 | | 3:00 | | 8:00 | |
| | 11:00 | | 4:00 | | 9:00 | |
| | 12:00 | | 5:00 | | 10:00 | |

Notes:

Priorities:

| Wednesday | | Morning | | Afternoon | | Evening |
|---|---|---|---|---|---|---|
| | 8:00 | | 1:00 | | 6:00 | |
| | 9:00 | | 2:00 | | 7:00 | |
| | 10:00 | | 3:00 | | 8:00 | |
| | 11:00 | | 4:00 | | 9:00 | |
| | 12:00 | | 5:00 | | 10:00 | |

Notes:

Priorities:

| Thursday | | Morning | | Afternoon | | Evening |
|---|---|---|---|---|---|---|
| | 8:00 | | 1:00 | | 6:00 | |
| | 9:00 | | 2:00 | | 7:00 | |
| | 10:00 | | 3:00 | | 8:00 | |
| | 11:00 | | 4:00 | | 9:00 | |
| | 12:00 | | 5:00 | | 10:00 | |

Notes:

Priorities:

| Friday | | Morning | | Afternoon | | Evening |
|---|---|---|---|---|---|---|
| | 8:00 | | 1:00 | | 6:00 | |
| | 9:00 | | 2:00 | | 7:00 | |
| | 10:00 | | 3:00 | | 8:00 | |
| | 11:00 | | 4:00 | | 9:00 | |
| | 12:00 | | 5:00 | | 10:00 | |

Notes:

Priorities:

| Weekend | | Morning | | Afternoon | | Evening |
|---|---|---|---|---|---|---|
| | 8:00 | | 1:00 | | 6:00 | |
| | 9:00 | | 2:00 | | 7:00 | |
| | 10:00 | | 3:00 | | 8:00 | |
| | 11:00 | | 4:00 | | 9:00 | |
| | 12:00 | | 5:00 | | 10:00 | |

Notes:

Priorities:

# Notes

# Week of: _____

| Monday | | Morning | | Afternoon | | Evening |
|---|---|---|---|---|---|---|
| | 8:00 | | 1:00 | | 6:00 | |
| | 9:00 | | 2:00 | | 7:00 | |
| | 10:00 | | 3:00 | | 8:00 | |
| | 11:00 | | 4:00 | | 9:00 | |
| | 12:00 | | 5:00 | | 10:00 | |

**Notes:**

**Priorities:**

| Tuesday | | Morning | | Afternoon | | Evening |
|---|---|---|---|---|---|---|
| | 8:00 | | 1:00 | | 6:00 | |
| | 9:00 | | 2:00 | | 7:00 | |
| | 10:00 | | 3:00 | | 8:00 | |
| | 11:00 | | 4:00 | | 9:00 | |
| | 12:00 | | 5:00 | | 10:00 | |

**Notes:**

**Priorities:**

| Wednesday | | Morning | | Afternoon | | Evening |
|---|---|---|---|---|---|---|
| | 8:00 | | 1:00 | | 6:00 | |
| | 9:00 | | 2:00 | | 7:00 | |
| | 10:00 | | 3:00 | | 8:00 | |
| | 11:00 | | 4:00 | | 9:00 | |
| | 12:00 | | 5:00 | | 10:00 | |

Notes:

Priorities:

| Thursday | | Morning | | Afternoon | | Evening |
|---|---|---|---|---|---|---|
| | 8:00 | | 1:00 | | 6:00 | |
| | 9:00 | | 2:00 | | 7:00 | |
| | 10:00 | | 3:00 | | 8:00 | |
| | 11:00 | | 4:00 | | 9:00 | |
| | 12:00 | | 5:00 | | 10:00 | |

Notes:

Priorities:

| Friday | | Morning | | Afternoon | | Evening |
|---|---|---|---|---|---|---|
| | 8:00 | | 1:00 | | 6:00 | |
| | 9:00 | | 2:00 | | 7:00 | |
| | 10:00 | | 3:00 | | 8:00 | |
| | 11:00 | | 4:00 | | 9:00 | |
| | 12:00 | | 5:00 | | 10:00 | |

Notes:

Priorities:

| Weekend | | Morning | | Afternoon | | Evening |
|---|---|---|---|---|---|---|
| | 8:00 | | 1:00 | | 6:00 | |
| | 9:00 | | 2:00 | | 7:00 | |
| | 10:00 | | 3:00 | | 8:00 | |
| | 11:00 | | 4:00 | | 9:00 | |
| | 12:00 | | 5:00 | | 10:00 | |

Notes:

Priorities:

## Notes

# Week of: _____

| Monday | | Morning | | Afternoon | | Evening |
|---|---|---|---|---|---|---|
| | 8:00 | | 1:00 | | 6:00 | |
| | 9:00 | | 2:00 | | 7:00 | |
| | 10:00 | | 3:00 | | 8:00 | |
| | 11:00 | | 4:00 | | 9:00 | |
| | 12:00 | | 5:00 | | 10:00 | |

Notes:

Priorities:

| Tuesday | | Morning | | Afternoon | | Evening |
|---|---|---|---|---|---|---|
| | 8:00 | | 1:00 | | 6:00 | |
| | 9:00 | | 2:00 | | 7:00 | |
| | 10:00 | | 3:00 | | 8:00 | |
| | 11:00 | | 4:00 | | 9:00 | |
| | 12:00 | | 5:00 | | 10:00 | |

Notes:

Priorities:

| Wednesday | | Morning | | Afternoon | | Evening |
|---|---|---|---|---|---|---|
| | 8:00 | | 1:00 | | 6:00 | |
| | 9:00 | | 2:00 | | 7:00 | |
| | 10:00 | | 3:00 | | 8:00 | |
| | 11:00 | | 4:00 | | 9:00 | |
| | 12:00 | | 5:00 | | 10:00 | |

Notes:

Priorities:

| Thursday | | Morning | | Afternoon | | Evening |
|---|---|---|---|---|---|---|
| | 8:00 | | 1:00 | | 6:00 | |
| | 9:00 | | 2:00 | | 7:00 | |
| | 10:00 | | 3:00 | | 8:00 | |
| | 11:00 | | 4:00 | | 9:00 | |
| | 12:00 | | 5:00 | | 10:00 | |

Notes:

Priorities:

| Friday | | Morning | | Afternoon | | Evening |
|---|---|---|---|---|---|---|
| | 8:00 | | 1:00 | | 6:00 | |
| | 9:00 | | 2:00 | | 7:00 | |
| | 10:00 | | 3:00 | | 8:00 | |
| | 11:00 | | 4:00 | | 9:00 | |
| | 12:00 | | 5:00 | | 10:00 | |

Notes:

Priorities:

| Weekend | | Morning | | Afternoon | | Evening |
|---|---|---|---|---|---|---|
| | 8:00 | | 1:00 | | 6:00 | |
| | 9:00 | | 2:00 | | 7:00 | |
| | 10:00 | | 3:00 | | 8:00 | |
| | 11:00 | | 4:00 | | 9:00 | |
| | 12:00 | | 5:00 | | 10:00 | |

Notes:

Priorities:

# Notes

# Week of: _____

| Monday | | Morning | | Afternoon | | Evening |
|---|---|---|---|---|---|---|
| | 8:00 | | 1:00 | | 6:00 | |
| | 9:00 | | 2:00 | | 7:00 | |
| | 10:00 | | 3:00 | | 8:00 | |
| | 11:00 | | 4:00 | | 9:00 | |
| | 12:00 | | 5:00 | | 10:00 | |

Notes:

Priorities:

| Tuesday | | Morning | | Afternoon | | Evening |
|---|---|---|---|---|---|---|
| | 8:00 | | 1:00 | | 6:00 | |
| | 9:00 | | 2:00 | | 7:00 | |
| | 10:00 | | 3:00 | | 8:00 | |
| | 11:00 | | 4:00 | | 9:00 | |
| | 12:00 | | 5:00 | | 10:00 | |

Notes:

Priorities:

## Wednesday

| | Morning | | Afternoon | | Evening |
|---|---|---|---|---|---|
| 8:00 | | 1:00 | | 6:00 | |
| 9:00 | | 2:00 | | 7:00 | |
| 10:00 | | 3:00 | | 8:00 | |
| 11:00 | | 4:00 | | 9:00 | |
| 12:00 | | 5:00 | | 10:00 | |

Notes:

Priorities:

## Thursday

| | Morning | | Afternoon | | Evening |
|---|---|---|---|---|---|
| 8:00 | | 1:00 | | 6:00 | |
| 9:00 | | 2:00 | | 7:00 | |
| 10:00 | | 3:00 | | 8:00 | |
| 11:00 | | 4:00 | | 9:00 | |
| 12:00 | | 5:00 | | 10:00 | |

Notes:

Priorities:

| Friday | | Morning | | Afternoon | | Evening |
|---|---|---|---|---|---|---|
| | 8:00 | | 1:00 | | 6:00 | |
| | 9:00 | | 2:00 | | 7:00 | |
| | 10:00 | | 3:00 | | 8:00 | |
| | 11:00 | | 4:00 | | 9:00 | |
| | 12:00 | | 5:00 | | 10:00 | |

Notes:

Priorities:

| Weekend | | Morning | | Afternoon | | Evening |
|---|---|---|---|---|---|---|
| | 8:00 | | 1:00 | | 6:00 | |
| | 9:00 | | 2:00 | | 7:00 | |
| | 10:00 | | 3:00 | | 8:00 | |
| | 11:00 | | 4:00 | | 9:00 | |
| | 12:00 | | 5:00 | | 10:00 | |

Notes:

Priorities:

# Notes

# Week of: _____

| Monday | | Morning | | Afternoon | | Evening |
|---|---|---|---|---|---|---|
| | 8:00 | | 1:00 | | 6:00 | |
| | 9:00 | | 2:00 | | 7:00 | |
| | 10:00 | | 3:00 | | 8:00 | |
| | 11:00 | | 4:00 | | 9:00 | |
| | 12:00 | | 5:00 | | 10:00 | |

**Notes:**

**Priorities:**

| Tuesday | | Morning | | Afternoon | | Evening |
|---|---|---|---|---|---|---|
| | 8:00 | | 1:00 | | 6:00 | |
| | 9:00 | | 2:00 | | 7:00 | |
| | 10:00 | | 3:00 | | 8:00 | |
| | 11:00 | | 4:00 | | 9:00 | |
| | 12:00 | | 5:00 | | 10:00 | |

**Notes:**

**Priorities:**

| Wednesday | | Morning | | Afternoon | | Evening |
|---|---|---|---|---|---|---|
| | 8:00 | | 1:00 | | 6:00 | |
| | 9:00 | | 2:00 | | 7:00 | |
| | 10:00 | | 3:00 | | 8:00 | |
| | 11:00 | | 4:00 | | 9:00 | |
| | 12:00 | | 5:00 | | 10:00 | |

Notes:

Priorities:

| Thursday | | Morning | | Afternoon | | Evening |
|---|---|---|---|---|---|---|
| | 8:00 | | 1:00 | | 6:00 | |
| | 9:00 | | 2:00 | | 7:00 | |
| | 10:00 | | 3:00 | | 8:00 | |
| | 11:00 | | 4:00 | | 9:00 | |
| | 12:00 | | 5:00 | | 10:00 | |

Notes:

Priorities:

| Friday | | Morning | | Afternoon | | Evening |
|---|---|---|---|---|---|---|
| | 8:00 | | 1:00 | | 6:00 | |
| | 9:00 | | 2:00 | | 7:00 | |
| | 10:00 | | 3:00 | | 8:00 | |
| | 11:00 | | 4:00 | | 9:00 | |
| | 12:00 | | 5:00 | | 10:00 | |

Notes:

Priorities:

| Weekend | | Morning | | Afternoon | | Evening |
|---|---|---|---|---|---|---|
| | 8:00 | | 1:00 | | 6:00 | |
| | 9:00 | | 2:00 | | 7:00 | |
| | 10:00 | | 3:00 | | 8:00 | |
| | 11:00 | | 4:00 | | 9:00 | |
| | 12:00 | | 5:00 | | 10:00 | |

Notes:

Priorities:

# Notes

Week of: _____

| Monday | | Morning | | Afternoon | | Evening |
|---|---|---|---|---|---|---|
| | 8:00 | | 1:00 | | 6:00 | |
| | 9:00 | | 2:00 | | 7:00 | |
| | 10:00 | | 3:00 | | 8:00 | |
| | 11:00 | | 4:00 | | 9:00 | |
| | 12:00 | | 5:00 | | 10:00 | |

Notes:

Priorities:

| Tuesday | | Morning | | Afternoon | | Evening |
|---|---|---|---|---|---|---|
| | 8:00 | | 1:00 | | 6:00 | |
| | 9:00 | | 2:00 | | 7:00 | |
| | 10:00 | | 3:00 | | 8:00 | |
| | 11:00 | | 4:00 | | 9:00 | |
| | 12:00 | | 5:00 | | 10:00 | |

Notes:

Priorities:

| Wednesday | | Morning | | Afternoon | | Evening |
|---|---|---|---|---|---|---|
| | 8:00 | | 1:00 | | 6:00 | |
| | 9:00 | | 2:00 | | 7:00 | |
| | 10:00 | | 3:00 | | 8:00 | |
| | 11:00 | | 4:00 | | 9:00 | |
| | 12:00 | | 5:00 | | 10:00 | |

Notes:

Priorities:

| Thursday | | Morning | | Afternoon | | Evening |
|---|---|---|---|---|---|---|
| | 8:00 | | 1:00 | | 6:00 | |
| | 9:00 | | 2:00 | | 7:00 | |
| | 10:00 | | 3:00 | | 8:00 | |
| | 11:00 | | 4:00 | | 9:00 | |
| | 12:00 | | 5:00 | | 10:00 | |

Notes:

Priorities:

| Friday | | Morning | | Afternoon | | Evening |
|---|---|---|---|---|---|---|
| | 8:00 | | 1:00 | | 6:00 | |
| | 9:00 | | 2:00 | | 7:00 | |
| | 10:00 | | 3:00 | | 8:00 | |
| | 11:00 | | 4:00 | | 9:00 | |
| | 12:00 | | 5:00 | | 10:00 | |

Notes:

Priorities:

| Weekend | | Morning | | Afternoon | | Evening |
|---|---|---|---|---|---|---|
| | 8:00 | | 1:00 | | 6:00 | |
| | 9:00 | | 2:00 | | 7:00 | |
| | 10:00 | | 3:00 | | 8:00 | |
| | 11:00 | | 4:00 | | 9:00 | |
| | 12:00 | | 5:00 | | 10:00 | |

Notes:

Priorities:

# Notes

# Notes

# Notes

# Contacts

Name:

Phone:

Address:

Email:

Name:

Phone:

Address:

Email:

Name:

Phone:

Address:

Email:

Name:

Phone:

Address:

Email:

Name:

Phone:

Address:

Email:

# Contacts

Name:

Phone:

Address:

Email:

Name:

Phone:

Address:

Email:

Name:

Phone:

Address:

Email:

Name:

Phone:

Address:

Email:

Name:

Phone:

Address:

Email:

To see our complete line of journals, planners, and notebooks visit:

ritchiemedia.ca

Follow Ritchie Media on:

Facebook.com/ritchiemedia

Instagram.com/ritchiemediaptbo

ritchie media, peterborough, on, canada

www.ingramcontent.com/pod-product-compliance
Lightning Source LLC
Chambersburg PA
CBHW082255220526
45469CB00009B/3018